My Life in a Book

A Journey ... A Memory ... A Keepsake

Created by: Stephanie Dipple

This Book belongs to:

_____

Date started this book:

_____

Date finished this book:

_____

Contents

Me, Myself & I

Full name:

Nickname(s):

Gender:

Date of birth:

Place of birth:

Time of birth:

Weight at birth:

Birth stone:

Star sign:

Nationality:

Religion:

Skin colour:

Eye colour:

Hair colour:

Height:

Weight:

Personality type:

Dress sense:

Sexuality:

Smoke?

Drink?

Relationship status:

Kids?

Motto:

Main language you speak:

Other languages you speak:

Named after anyone:

10 Facts about me

1.

2.

3.

4.

5.

6.

7.

8.

9.

10.

My Personality traits

[Circle your personality traits]

Positive traits

Active
Adventurous
Athletic
Brave
Challenging
Competent
Clean
Caring
Confident
Clever
Creative
Dramatic
Energetic
Easy going
Entertaining
Enthusiastic
Fair
Forgiving
Faithful
Funny
Generous
Glamorous
Hard working
Healthy
Happy
Helpful
Honest
Imaginative
Innocent

Kind
Loyal
Mannered
Organised
Open minded
Passionate
Patient
Perfectionist
Quirky
Romantic
Reliable
Responsible
Realistic
Secure
Selfless
Selfish
Sensitive
Sharing
Successful
Simple
Smart
Strong
Sensible
Spontaneous
Sociable
Talented
Sweet
Tidy
Thoughtful
Trusting
Understanding

Negative traits

Aggressive
Absent minded
Anxious
Abrupt
Bossy
Boring
Childish
Competitive
Cold hearted
Clumsy
Disorganised
Envious
Forgetful
Greedy
Gullible
Hesitant
Insecure
Ignorant
Indulgent
Impatient
Irresponsible
Lazy
Naive
Obsessive
Opinionated
Paranoid
Quiet
Reserved
Sarcastic
Serious
Stubborn
Secretive
Shy
Stupid

My Body

Tattoos:

Piercing's:

Birth marks:

Ring size:

Shoe size:

Clothes size:

Left or right handed:

Long or short finger nails:

Stitches:

Broken bones:

Scars:

Shave:

Favourite body part:

Not so favourite body part:

Dyed hair colour:

Hair style:

Hair texture:

Wear make - up:

Wear jewellery:

Painted nails:

Skin conditions:

Glasses:

Allergies:

Freckles:

Skin type:

Things I like about myself

1.

2.

3.

4.

5.

6.

7.

8.

9.

10.

Things I don't like about myself

1.

2.

3.

4.

5.

6.

7.

8.

9.

10.

Home

Where do you currently live:

What kind of area do you live in:

What type of home do you live in:

Who do you live with:

What is your home like:

Must have items in your home:

What sort of home deco do you have:

You like your home to smell like:

What colour is each room -

Living room:

Kitchen:

Bath room:

Bed room:

Children's bed room:

Hall way:

Other rooms:

How many times have you moved home:

Types of homes you've lived in:

Previous addresses:

....

....

....

....

....

....

....

....

....

....

....

....

....

Family & Pets

Family name:

<u>Parents</u> -

Mother's name: D.O.B:

Father's name: D.O.B:

Mother's maiden name:

Parents still together?

Parents married?

<u>Siblings</u> -

Brother's name: D.O.B:

Brother's name: D.O.B:

Brother's name: D.O.B:

Brother's name: D.O.B:

Sister's name: D.O.B:

Sister's name: D.O.B:

Sister's name: D.O.B:

Sister's name: D.O.B:

<u>Partner</u> -   D.O.B:

<u>Children</u> -

Name: D.O.B:

Name: D.O.B:

Name: D.O.B:

Name: D.O.B:

Name: D.O.B:

Name: D.O.B:

<u>Pets</u> -

Animal: Name:

Animal: Name:

Animal: Name:

Animal: Name:

Animal: Name:

Animal: Name:

Animal: Name:

Animal: Name:

Pets you've had –

....

....

....

....

....

....

....

....

....

....

....

....

....

....

....

....

Family Tree

My Partner

Name:

Date of birth:

Date you met:

....

How you met:

....

....

....

Where you met:

....

....

First date:

....

....

First kiss:

....

....

First time slept together:

....

....

Personality:

....

....

....

....

....

Hair style:

....

Dress sense:

....

Physical feature:

....

....

....

Joint bank account?

....

Hobbies and Interests:

....

....

....

Living together?   Date:

First pet together?   Date:

Engaged?   Date:

Married?   Date:

Kids together? -

Name: Born:

Name: Born:

Name: Born:

Name: Born:

Name: Born:

Name: Born:

Describe the relationship:

....

....

....

....

....

....

....

....

....

....

....

....

....

....

....

....

My Children

1st Child's name:

D.O.B:

Hair colour:

Eye colour:

Time of birth:

Weight at birth:

Favourites -

Tv shows:

....

....

....

....

Music:

....

....

....

....

Books:

....

....

....

....

Food & Drink:

....

....

....

....

Movies:

....

....

....

....

Hobbies & Interests:

....

....

....

2nd Child's name:

D.O.B:

Hair colour:

Eye colour:

Time of birth:

Weight at birth:

Favourites -

Tv shows:

....

....

....

....

....

Music:

....

....

....

....

....

Books:

....

....

....

....

Food & Drink:

....

....

....

....

Movies:

....

....

....

....

Hobbies & Interests:

....

....

....

3rd Child's name:

D.O.B:

Hair colour:

Eye colour:

Time of birth:

Weight at birth:

Favourites -

Tv shows:

....

....

....

....

....

Music:

....

....

....

....

....

Books:

....

....

....

....

Food & Drink:

....

....

....

....

Movies:

....

....

....

....

Hobbies & Interests:

....

....

....

4th Child's name:

D.O.B:

Hair colour:

Eye colour:

Time of birth:

Weight at birth:

Favourites -

Tv shows:

....

....

....

....

....

Music:

....

....

....

....

....

Books:

....

....

....

....

Food & Drink:

....

....

....

....

Movies:

....

....

....

....

Hobbies & Interests:

....

....

....

5th Child's name:

D.O.B:

Hair colour:

Eye colour:

Time of birth:

Weight at birth:

Favourites -

Tv shows:

....

....

....

....

....

Music:

....

....

....

....

....

Books:

....

....

....

....

Food & Drink:

....

....

....

Movies:

....

....

....

....

Hobbies & Interests:

....

....

....

6th Child's name:

D.O.B:

Hair colour:

Eye colour:

Time of birth:

Weight at birth:

Favourites -

Tv shows:

....

....

....

....

....

Music:

....

....

....

....

....

Books:

....

....

....

....

Food & Drink:

....

....

....

....

Movies:

....

....

....

....

Hobbies & Interests:

....

....

....

If you don't have Children -

Do you want Children?

What age would you want them:

How many Children do you want:

Names you like:

....

....

....

....

....

....

....

....

....

Friends

Best friend:

Work friend:

Longest friend:

Current friends –

....

....

....

....

....

....

Past friends –

....

....

....

....

....

My Star sign

Your Star sign:

Your Star sign describes you as:

....

....

....

....

....

....

....

....

....

....

....

....

....

Favourites

Colour:

Animal:

Pet:

Book:

Movie:

TV show:

Female singer:

Male singer:

Female band:

Male band:

Sport:

Magazine:

Newspaper:

Holiday:

Girl's name:

Boy's name:

Age:

Hot food:

Cold food:

Hot drink:

Cold drink:

Alcohol:

Actress:

Actor:

Football team:

Flower:

Season:

Day of the week:

Month:

Time of day:

Number:

Letter:

Shape:

Writing topic:

Technology:

Hobby:

Gem stone:

Type of weather:

Perfume/Cologne:

Game:

Board game:

Car:

Outfit:

Shop:

Type of shop:

Celebrity:

Website:

Blog:

Time to get up:

Time to go bed:

Place to shop:

Plant:

Tree:

Joke:

Instrument:

Day of the year:

Form of entertainment:

Type of house chores:

Morning activity:

Evening activity:

Quote:

Least Favourites

Colour:

Animal:

Pet:

Book:

Movie:

TV show:

Female singer:

Male singer:

Female band:

Male band:

Sport:

Magazine:

Newspaper:

Holiday:

Girl's name:

Boy's name:

Age:

Hot food:

Cold food:

Hot drink:

Cold drink:

Alcohol:

Actress:

Actor:

Football team:

Flower:

Season:

Day of the week:

Month:

Time of day:

Number:

Letter:

Shape:

Writing topic:

Technology:

Hobby:

Gem stone:

Type of weather:

Perfume/Cologne:

Game:

Board game:

Car:

Outfit:

Shop:

Type of shop:

Celebrity:

Website:

Blog:

Time to get up:

Time to go bed:

Place to shop:

Plant:

Tree:

Joke:

Instrument:

Day of the year:

Form of entertainment:

Type of house chores:

Morning activity:

Evening activity:

Quote:

Hobbies & Interests

1.

2.

3.

4.

5.

6.

7.

8.

9.

10.

11.

12.

13.

14.

15.

I LOVE...

....

....

....

....

....

....

....

....

....

....

....

....

....

....

....

....

....

....

I HATE...

....

....

....

....

....

....

....

....

....

....

....

....

....

....

....

....

Life goals

1.

2.

3.

4.

5.

6.

7.

8.

9.

10.

Beliefs

Do you believe in -

Ghosts:
Evolution:
Aliens:
Superstitions:
Karma:
After life:
God:
Life on other planets:
Love at first sight:
Miracles:
Heaven:
Hell:
Reincarnation:
Hypnosis:
Psychics:
Angels:
Demons:
Fairies:
Witchcraft:
That everything happens for a reason:
Fate:
Soul mates:
Sex before marriage:
Unicorns:
Voodoo:
Healing crystals:

Worst fears

1.

2.

3.

4.

5.

6.

7.

8.

9.

10.

Work

Current Job:

Date started:

Hours per week:

Wage:

<u>Jobs you've had</u> -

Name of Job:
Date started:
Date finished:
Reason Job finished:

Name of Job:
Date started:
Date finished:
Reason Job finished:

Name of Job:
Date started:
Date finished:
Reason Job finished:

Name of Job:
Date started:
Date finished:
Reason Job finished:

Jobs you'd love to have –

....

....

....

....

....

....

....

....

....

....

....

....

....

....

....

Travel

Favourite places you've been:

....

....

....

....

....

....

....

....

....

....

....

....

....

....

Holidays you've been on -

By plane:

....

....

....

By car:

....

....

....

By ferry:

....

....

....

Other:

....

....

....

....

....

Travelled by car?

Travelled by plane?

Travelled by ferry?

Been in a limo?

Been on a train?

Been in a boat?

Been on a ship?

Been on a helicopter?

Been in a submarine?

Been on a cruise?

Been on a road trip?

Do you drive?

Current car:

Previous cars you've owned:

....

....

....

__Child hood__

What was you like as a child:

....

....

Child hood friends:

....

....

....

....

Favourite games:

....

....

....

Favourite toys:

....

....

....

....

Favourite teddy bear:

....

....

Fashion:

....

....

....

Hair style:

....

Worst hair cuts:

....

....

What did you want to be when you were older:

....

Favourite TV shows:

....

....

....

....

Favourite movies:

....

....

....

....

Favourite music:

....

....

....

....

Favourite books:

....

....

....

....

Favourite food:

....

....

....

Day trips been on:

....

....

....

....

Holidays:

....

....

....

Favourite outdoor games:

....

....

....

Camping days:

....

....

....

Personality:

....

....

....

....

Share a room with siblings?

....

....

Change your room?

....

....

What was your bed room like:

....

....

....

....

Close to your cousins?

....

....

School

Primary school:

Year started Primary school:

Year finished Primary school:

Best friends:

....

....

....

....

....

Boyfriends/Girlfriends:

....

....

....

....

Subjects enjoyed:

....

....

....

....

Subjects didn't enjoy:

....

....

....

....

Favourite playground games:

....

....

....

....

Trends at school:

....

....

....

Secondary school:

Year started Secondary school:

Year finished Secondary school:

Best friends:

....

....

....

....

....

....

Boyfriends/Girlfriends:

....

....

....

....

....

Subjects enjoyed:

....

....

....

....

Subjects didn't enjoy:

....

....

....

....

Favourite playground games:

....

....

....

....

Trends at school:

....

....

....

Teens

What was you like as a Teenager:

....

....

....

Best friends:

....

....

....

....

....

Boyfriends/Girlfriends:

....

....

....

....

....

What was your bed room like:

....

....

....

Hobbies and Interests:

....

....

....

....

Personality:

....

....

....

....

What age did you start wearing Make-up:

....

Fashion:

....

....

Hair styles:

....

....

....

Did you have sleep overs?

....

....

Favourite TV shows:

....

....

....

....

....

Favourite Movies:

....

....

....

....

....

Favourite Books:

....

....

....

....

....

Favourite Music:

....

....

....

....

....

Favourite Games:

....

....

....

....

....

....

Dating/Relationships

Relationships been in:

....

....

....

Longest relationship:

....

Shortest relationship:

....

Been cheated on:

....

....

Cheated on:

....

....

Ever been on a brake:

....

....

Had an open relationship:

....

....

Had a long distance relationship:

....

....

Been on a double date:

....

....

Been on a blind date:

....

....

Got rejected:

....

....

Been in love:

....

....

How many times have you been in love:

Attracted to older or younger people:

....

....

What type of men/women do you go for:

....

....

Kissed:

....

....

....

....

Slept with:

....

....

....

....

Best date:

....

....

Worst date:

....

....

Kissed a stranger?

Kissed the same sex?

Turns on:

....

....

....

Turns off:

....

....

....

What do you find romantic:

....

....

Compliments you've received:

....

....

....

Reasons to end a relationship:

....

....

....

....

Ideal partner:

....

....

....

....

Favourite features:

....

....

....

....

Favourite place to go on a date:

....

....

....

Flowers you would like to receive:

....

....

Favourite kind of kiss:

....

....

Favourite place to be kissed:

....

....

Favourite topic of conversation:

....

....

Way to show affection:

....

....

What a relationship should have:

....

....

....

....

....

....

....

....

....

....

....

....

....

....

....

....

Ex Boyfriends/Girlfriends

Name   Relationship lasted   Reason ended

....

....

....

....

....

....

....

....

....

....

....

....

....

....

....

Being grateful

Smells you love:

....

....

....

....

....

....

....

Tastes you love:

....

....

....

....

....

....

....

Sights you love:

....

....

....

....

....

....

....

....

Sounds you love:

....

....

....

....

....

....

....

....

Hobbies I've done/tried

1.

2.

3.

4.

5.

6.

7.

8.

9.

10.

11.

12.

13.

14.

15.

16.

17.

18.

19.

20.

Hobbies I want to try

1.

2.

3.

4.

5.

6.

7.

8.

9.

10.

11.

12.

13.

14.

15.

16.

17.

18.

19.

20.

Things I'd like to learn...

1.

2.

3.

4.

5.

6.

7.

8.

9.

10.

11.

12.

13.

14.

15.

16.

17.

18.

19.

20.

Bucket list

Things to do:

....

....

....

....

....

....

....

....

....

....

....

....

....

....

Things to make:

....

....

....

....

....

....

....

....

....

....

....

....

....

....

....

....

Places to go:

....

....

....

....

....

....

....

....

....

....

....

....

....

....

....

....

....

Memories

Earliest memory:

....

....

....

....

Childhood memories:

....

....

....

....

....

Teen memories:

....

....

....

....

....

Happy memories:

....

....

....

....

....

School memories:

....

....

....

....

....

Family memories:

....

....

....

....

....

....

Favourite memories with your Mum:

....

....

....

....

....

....

....

....

Favourite memories with your Dad:

....

....

....

....

....

....

....

....

Dreams

Weirdest dream you've had:

....

....

....

Funniest dream you've had:

....

....

....

Happiest dream you've had:

....

....

....

....

A dream that made you cry when you woke up:

....

....

....

A dream that made you wake up in a panic:

....

....

....

....

A dream that made you smile:

....

....

....

....

A dream that made you worried:

....

....

....

A dream that seemed so real:

....

....

....

....

Talents

1.

2.

3.

4.

5.

6.

7.

8.

9.

10.

<u>Achievements</u>

1.

2.

3.

4.

5.

6.

7.

8.

9.

10.

I am grateful for...

1.

2.

3.

4.

5.

6.

7.

8.

9.

10.

Creativity

Things you've made that you're proud of:

....

....

....

....

....

....

....

Things you've made that you're disappointed at:

....

....

....

....

....

....

....

Collections

I collect:

....

....

....

....

....

....

....

....

....

....

....

....

....

....

....

<u>What's in my bag</u>

1.

2.

3.

4.

5.

6.

7.

8.

9.

10.

11.

12.

13.

14.

15.

16.

17.

18.

19.

20.

Routines

Morning routine:

....

....

....

....

....

....

....

Evening routine:

....

....

....

....

....

....

....

Weekly routine:

....

....

....

....

....

....

....

....

Monthly routine:

....

....

....

....

....

....

....

Places to visit

1.

2.

3.

4.

5.

6.

7.

8.

9.

10.

11.

12.

13.

14.

15.

16.

17.

18.

19.

20.

What makes me happy

1.

2.

3.

4.

5.

6.

7.

8.

9.

10.

<u>What inspires me!</u>

1.

2.

3.

4.

5.

6.

7.

8.

9.

10.

Who do I admire?

Name:

Reasons why?

1.

2.

3.

4.

5.

<u>Wish list</u>

1.

2.

3.

4.

5.

6.

7.

8.

9.

10.

11.

12.

13.

14.

15.

My Life in A – Z

A

....

....

B

....

....

C

....

....

D

....

....

E

....

....

F

....

....

G

....

....

H

....

....

I

....

....

J

....

....

K

....

....

L

....

....

M

....

....

N

....

....

O

....

....

P

....

....

Q

....

....

R

....

....

S

....

....

T

....

....

U

....

....

V

....

....

W

....

....

X

....

....

Y

....

....

Z

....

....

Thoughts/Views on...

Love:

....

....

....

Smoking:

....

....

....

Death penalty:

....

....

....

Marriage:

....

....

....

Politics:

....

....

....

Internet:

....

....

....

Positive thinking:

....

....

....

Divorce:

....

....

....

Being a vegetarian:

....

....

....

Pregnancy:

....

....

....

One night stands:

....

....

....

Make - up:

....

....

....

Gambling:

....

....

....

Adoption:

....

....

....

Drugs:

....

....

....

Alcohol:

....

....

....

Home remedies:

....

....

....

The bible:

....

....

....

Plastic surgery:

....

....

....

Tattoos:

....

....

....

Organ donating:

....

....

....

Cheating:

....

....

....

Hunting:

....

....

....

The news:

....

....

....

Recycling:

....

....

....

Nude photography:

....

....

....

Organic food:

....

....

....

Soul mates:

....

....

....

Parenting:

....

....

....

Evolution:

....

....

....

Abortion:

....

....

....

Fur coats:

....

....

....

Food waste:

....

....

....

Animal testing:

....

....

....

Buses:

....

....

....

If I were rich...

Things you would buy:

....

....

....

....

Places you would go:

....

....

....

....

Things you would do:

....

....

....

....

The World needs...

_____

Changes you would make:

....

....

....

....

....

....

....

....

....

....

....

....

....

The Perfect me

Changes you would make to your body:

....

....

....

....

....

....

....

Changes you would make to your personality:

....

....

....

....

....

....

....

My Dream home

Type of home:

Location:

Colour of the rooms -

Bed room:

Living room:

Kitchen:

Bath room:

Children's bed room:

Hall way:

Other:

Bed room -

Walls:

Deco:

Type of furniture:

Layout:

Living room -

Walls:

Deco:

Type of furniture:

Layout:

Kitchen -

Walls:

Deco:

Type of furniture:

Layout:

Bath room -

Walls:

Deco:

Type of furniture:

Layout:

Child's bed room -

Walls:

Deco:

Type of furniture:

Layout:

Garden -

The Best birthdays ever

....

....

....

....

....

....

....

....

....

....

....

....

....

....

....

....

....

Recipes

Favourite recipes that you've tried:

....

....

....

....

....

....

....

Recipes you want to try:

....

....

....

....

....

....

....

My Wedding day

Date got married:

How long been together before getting married:

What was the proposal like:

Morning of the wedding day:

After noon of the wedding day:

Evening of the wedding day:

My Dream wedding

Bride's dress:

Groom's tux:

Theme:

Location of wedding:

Location of party:

Honey moon location:

Bridesmaids:

Type of flowers & colour:

Centerpieces:

Favours:

Cake:

Type of food:

Type of music:

Decorations:

Entertainment:

Transport:

Hair:

Make - up:

Photography:

Guest book:

Reasons why I Love...

....

-
-
-
-
-
-
-
-
-
-
-
-
-

<u>Reasons why I Love...</u>

....

-
-
-
-
-
-
-
-
-
-
-
-
-

Moments

Happy moments:

....

....

....

....

....

....

....

Sad moments:

....

....

....

....

....

....

....

Angry moments:

....

....

....

....

Embarrassing moments:

....

....

....

....

....

Funny moments:

....

....

....

....

....

What makes me...

Happy...

....

....

....

....

....

Sad...

....

....

....

....

Stress out...

....

....

....

....

Angry...

....

....

....

....

....

Embarrassed...

....

....

....

....

Cry...

....

....

....

....

....

....

First's

First pet:

First home:

First kiss:

First date:

First french kiss:

First time slept with someone:

First word:

First Job:

First love:

First car:

First concert:

First best friend:

First boyfriend/girlfriend:

First time clubbing:

First steps:

First thing you do each morning:

Interested in...

Sports?
Science?
History?
Cultures?
Fashion?
Make-up?
Writing?
Animals?
Music?
Cooking?
Baking?
Gardening?
Gadgets?
Politics?
Philosophy?
Singing?
Dancing?
Painting?
Drawing?
Fighting?
Random facts?
Dinosaurs?
Journaling?
The big bang theory?
Sightseeing?
Photography?
Having a family?
Acting?

When I'm...

When I'm happy...

....

....

....

....

....

When I'm sad...

....

....

....

....

When I'm angry...

....

....

....

....

When I'm stressed...

....

....

....

....

....

When I'm in love...

....

....

....

....

When I'm nervous...

....

....

....

....

Can you...?

Can you make decisions?

Can you do the splits?

Can you swim?

Can you remember peoples birthdays?

Can you sleep on both sides?

Can you write with both hands?

Can you keep secrets?

Can you do hand stands?

Can you do head stands?

Can you control your temper?

Can you show your emotions?

Can you use a compass?

Can you whistle?

Can you sing?

Can you dance?

Can you draw?

Can you paint?

Can you read maps?

Can you walk in high heels?

Can you type fast?

Can you run fast?

Can you ice skate?

Can you roller skate?

Can you cook?

Can you spell big words?

Can you touch your nose with your tongue?

Can you roll your tongue in a circle?

Can you eat a lot without gaining weight?

Can you play an instrument?

Can you blow bubbles with gum?

Can you fall asleep right when you go to bed?

Do you...?

Do you read in the bath room?

Do you want children?

Do you swear?

Do you lose things?

Do you vote?

Do you sing in the shower?

Do you use coasters for your cups?

Do you pluck your eyebrows?

Do you think pregnancy is amazing?

Do you keep a Journal?

Do you want to get married?

Do you bruise easily?

Do you have an OCD?

Do you snore?

Do you keep a Planner?

Do you remember your dreams?

Do you talk in your sleep?

Do you scrub your tongue when brushing your teeth?

Do you sleep walk?

Do you recycle?

Do you save your birthday cards?

Do you have a memory keepsake box?

Do you wear a watch?

Do you eat when you're bored?

Do you get travel sickness?

Do you speak your mind?

Do you think before you speak?

Do you bite your nails?

Do you like being centre of attention?

Do you carry cash on you?

Do you take any vitamins?

Have you...?

Have you had braces?

Have you eaten sushi?

Have you had a pen pal?

Have you got children?

Have you been on a tanning bed?

Have you been in an car accident?

Have you ate raw meat?

Have you ever fainted?

Have you been stung by a bee?

Have you won a contest?

Have you been baptized?

Have you ever waxed your body?

Have you ever seen a shooting star?

Have you ever performed on stage?

Have you ever broken a bone?

Have you ever been stalked?

Have you gone a whole day without eating?

Have you felt an earthquake?

Have you ever been on a diet and kept to it?

Have you ever won anything?

Have you cried yourself to sleep?

Have you ever laughed so hard that you cried?

Have you kissed in the rain?

Have you danced in the rain?

Have you stayed in your bed all day?

Have you stayed in all day and just watched Tv?

Have you read a whole book in one day?

Have you ever kept track of the calories you eat?

Have you ever met someone famous?

Have you ever skipped school?

Have you ever experienced déjà vu?

This or that

hot or cold

credit or cash

read or write

smoke or drink

tv or radio

dance or sing

e-mails or letters

cats or dogs

phone or text

incense or candles

country or city

love or money

coffee or tea

shower or bath

morning or evening

diet or exercise

chocolate or sweets

salt or pepper

vegetables or fruit

tattoos or piercing's

shower am or shower pm

toast or cereal

book or movie

sunny or snow

christmas or birthday

curtains or blinds

cuddles or kisses

curly fries or french fries

pepsi or coke

red wine or white wine

silver or gold

blue jeans or black jeans

white tea or black tea

ice cream or milk shake

hearts or stars

honey or jam

Favourite Brands

Toothpaste:

Shampoo:

Make - up:

Skin product:

Stationary:

Nail polish:

Pen:

Planner/Organiser:

Furniture:

Phone:

Clothes:

Shoes:

Jewellery:

Body spray:

Perfume/Cologne:

Hair spray/Hair gel:

Computer:

Console:

Bag:

Purse/Wallet:

Chocolate:

Candle:

Car:

Sports wear:

Watch:

<u>**Movies**</u>

Favourite type of movie:

Favourite cartoon character:

Favourite disney character:

Favourite disney movie:

Favourite quote from movie:

Favourite Actress:

Favourite Actor:

Favourite thriller movie:

Favourite comedy movie:

Favourite horror movie:

Favourite crime movie:

Favourite family movie:

Favourite children's movie:

Favourite action movie:

Favourite romance movie:

Favourite chick flick movie:

Favourite sci-fi movie:

Favourite musical movie:

Favourite short movie:

Favourite romantic scene:

Favourite funny scene:

Movie that made you cry:

Movie that made you laugh:

Movie that made you feel good:

Movie that made you fall asleep:

Movie you can watch over and over again:

Favourite disney princess:

Favourite disney prince:

Favourite disney villain:

Favourite disney animal:

Favourite movie of all time:

Worst movie ever seen:

A few of your favourite movies:

TV shows

Favourite type of TV show:

Favourite cartoon character:

Favourite quote from TV show:

Favourite Actress:

Favourite Actor:

Favourite comedian:

Favourite chef:

Favourite sports person:

Favourite documentary:

Favourite reality show:

Favourite game show:

Favourite drama:

Favourite soap:

Favourite comedy show:

Favourite cooking show:

Favourite stand - up comedy show:

Favourite crime show:

Favourite children's show:

Favourite family show:

Favourite talk show:

Favourite cartoon:

Favourite type of sports to watch:

Favourite TV series:

Have you seen every episode of a TV show?

Favourite TV show of all time:

Worst TV show of all time:

A few of your favourite TV shows:

Books

Favourite book character:

Favourite Author:

Favourite type of books:

Favourite magazine:

Favourite newspaper:

Favourite thriller book:

Favourite romance book:

Favourite comedy book:

Favourite crime book:

Favourite children's book:

Favourite activity book:

Favourite mystery book:

Favourite fantasy book:

Favourite horror book:

Favourite non - fiction book:

Favourite fiction book:

Favourite self help book:

Favourite autobiography:

Favourite cook book:

Favourite short story:

Favourite comic:

Favourite fairy tale:

Favourite poem:

Favourite Artist:

Favourite Illustrator:

Favourite series of books:

Favourite book of all time:

Type of Journals you keep:

Music

Favourite genre of music:

Favourite radio station:

Favourite song writer:

Favourite concert:

Favourite way to listen to music:

Favourite lyrics:

Favourite song:

Favourite album:

Favourite music TV channel:

Favourite soundtrack:

Favourite TV theme:

Favourite female singer:

Favourite male singer:

Favourite female band:

Favourite male band:

Favourite mixed band:

Favourite musical:

Favourite type of dance:

Any songs you know the words to by heart:

Favourite pop singer/band:

Favourite rap singer/band:

Favourite country singer/band:

Favourite rock singer/band:

Favourite R&B singer/band:

Most annoying song:

Worst song ever heard:

Worst album ever brought:

Worst singer:

Worst band:

Songs

Songs you listen to when your...

Happy:

....

....

....

....

....

....

....

Sad:

....

....

....

....

....

....

....

Lonely:

....

....

....

....

....

In the mood to dance:

....

....

....

....

Cleaning:

....

....

....

....

....

Running:

....

....

....

....

....

Exercising:

....

....

....

....

....

Getting ready to go clubbing:

....

....

....

....

....

....

Feeling sexy:

....

....

....

....

....

Driving:

....

....

....

....

....

Heart broken:

....

....

....

....

....

....

Getting ready to go out:

....

....

....

....

....

Feeling good:

....

....

....

....

....

Feeling relaxed:

....

....

....

....

....

....

Favourite songs

Favourite romantic song:

Favourite feel good song:

Favourite party song:

Favourite wedding song:

Favourite dance song:

Favourite clubbing song:

Favourite disney song:

Favourite R&B song:

Favourite rap song:

Favourite reggae song:

Favourite pop song:

Favourite rock song:

Favourite jazz song:

Favourite love song:

Favourite christmas song:

Favourite nursery rhyme:

Favourite lullaby:

Favourite chilled out song:

Favourite karaoke song:

Favourite 50's song:

Favourite 60's song:

Favourite 70's song:

Favourite 80's song:

Favourite 90's song:

Favourite 2000's song:

Favourite chart song:

Perfect play list

1.

2.

3.

4.

5.

6.

7.

8.

9.

10.

Games

Favourite board game:

Favourite party game:

Favourite travel game:

Favourite arcade game:

Favourite console game:

Favourite video game:

Favourite PC game:

Favourite children's game:

Favourite creative game:

Favourite computer game:

Favourite mini game:

Favourite mobile game:

Favourite drinking game:

Favourite card game:

Favourite dice game:

Favourite pencil and paper game:

Favourite strategy game:

Favourite puzzle game:

Favourite quiz game:

Favourite word game:

Type of computer you use:

Type of console you use:

Favourite game of all time:

A few of your favourite games:

The Internet

Your website:

Your blog:

Topics you write about:

Your shop online:

Online shops you love:

Blogs you enjoy reading:

Website's you love:

Social networks you use:

Search engine you use:

Kind of computer you use:

Apps you love:

....

....

....

....

....

....

....

....

....

....

....

....

....

....

....

....

Animals

Favourite animal:

Favourite animal that lives in water:

Favourite wild animal:

Favourite insect:

Favourite bird:

Favourite four legged animal:

Favourite two legged animal:

Favourite reptile:

Favourite farm animal:

Favourite amphibian:

Favourite animal that lives in the arctic:

Favourite fish:

Favourite mammal:

Favourite cat breed:

Favourite dog breed:

Favourite animal that you can have as a pet:

Favourite sea creature:

Favourite flying creature:

Favourite dinosaur:

Favourite desert animal:

Animals you don't like:

Favourite names for pets:

Pets you would like to have:

Fashion

Favourite clothes shop:

Favourite type of clothes:

Favourite type of shoes:

Favourite designer:

Favourite outfit:

Favourite type of jewellery:

Favourite earrings:

Favourite necklace:

Favourite bracelet:

Favourite ring:

Favourite shoes:

Favourite dress:

Favourite suite:

Favourite jacket/coat:

Favourite bag:

Favourite top:

Favourite bottoms:

Favourite pyjamas:

Favourite slippers:

Favourite hat:

Favourite watch:

Favourite swimsuit:

Favourite fancy dress:

Favourite type of material/fabric:

Favourite pattern on clothes:

Favourite colour that suits me:

Beauty

Favourite brand hair dye:

Favourite colour hair dye:

Favourite bubble bath:

Favourite shampoo:

Favourite perfume/cologne:

Favourite coloured contact lenses:

Favourite hair style:

Favourite foundation:

Favourite eye shadow:

Favourite mascara:

Favourite eye liner:

Favourite blusher:

Favourite lip balm:

Favourite lip gloss:

Favourite lip stick:

Favourite lip liner:

Favourite face primer:

Favourite concealer:

Favourite face powder:

Favourite nail polish:

Favourite lipstick colour:

Favourite lip gloss colour:

Favourite eye shadow colour:

Favourite nail polish colour:

Favourite foundation shade:

Favourite bronzer:

Favourite hair tool:

Favourite deodorant:

Favourite hair spray/hair gel:

Favourite hair mask:

Favourite face mask:

Favourite face wash:

Favourite skin product:

Favourite face scrub:

Favourite face cream:

Favourite hand cream:

Favourite eye cream:

Favourite moisturizer:

Favourite face toner:

Favourite make - up product:

Favourite make - up remover:

Favourite hair product:

Favourite facial wipes:

Favourite beauty shop:

Worst beauty product:

Any falseness:

Beauty routine:

Food

Favourite food:

Favourite junk food:

Favourite breakfast:

Favourite dinner:

Favourite pudding:

Favourite snack:

Favourite lunch:

Favourite meat:

Favourite pasta dish:

Favourite sandwich:

Favourite sweets:

Favourite chocolate:

Favourite type of chocolate:

Favourite salad:

Favourite fruit:

Favourite vegetable:

Favourite biscuit:

Favourite pie:

Favourite cake:

Favourite soup:

Favourite taste:

Favourite fast food:

Favourite restaurant:

Favourite gum:

Favourite gravy:

Favourite mint:

Favourite rice:

Favourite flavour jelly bean:

Favourite topping on toast:

Favourite curry dish:

Favourite dairy product:

Favourite bread:

Favourite meal of the day:

Favourite flavour:

Favourite spice:

Favourite herb:

Favourite boiled sweets:

Favourite seasoning:

Favourite crisps:

Favourite condiment:

Favourite popcorn flavour:

Favourite nationality of food:

Favourite cereal:

Favourite salad dressing:

Favourite meal to cook:

Favourite burger:

Favourite jam:

Favourite chinese dish:

Favourite italian dish:

Favourite mexican dish:

Favourite american dish:

Favourite indian dish:

Favourite english dish:

Favourite fish:

Favourite type of pastry:

Favourite type of eggs:

Favourite sea food:

Favourite ice - cream:

Favourite pizza topping:

Favourite potato type:

Favourite midnight snack:

Favourite yogurt:

Foods I hate:

Perfect menu

....

....

....

....

....

....

....

....

....

Drink

Favourite drink:

Favourite hot drink:

Favourite cold drink:

Favourite comfort drink:

Favourite christmas drink:

Favourite milk shake:

Favourite tea bags:

Favourite coffee brand:

Favourite coffee flavour:

Favourite tea flavour:

Favourite hot chocolate brand:

Favourite soft drink:

Favourite alcohol drink:

Favourite fizzy drink:

Favourite water flavour:

Favourite type of water:

Favourite juice:

Favourite slushie:

Favourite cocktail:

Favourite smoothie:

Favourite wine:

How do you like your tea?

How do you like your coffee?

White or brown sugar?

Whole milk or semi - skimmed milk?

Do you ever drink with a straw?

Do you like other people making your tea/coffee?

Do you put the milk in first or water in first?

Do you dip the biscuits in your tea?

Drinks I hate:

<u>What I keep in my Memory keepsake box</u>

-
-
-
-
-
-
-
-
-
-
-
-
-
-

What's inside my Planner/Organiser...

-
-
-
-
-
-
-
-
-
-
-
-
-
-

Best things about being a child?

....

....

....

....

....

....

....

....

Best things about being an adult?

....

....

....

....

....

....

....

....

Things I can't live without

....

....

....

....

....

....

....

....

Things I never leave home without

....

....

....

....

....

....

....

....

Reasons to start...

_____

....

....

....

....

....

....

....

Reasons to quit...

_____

....

....

....

....

....

....

....

Best feelings in the world...

....

....

....

....

....

....

....

....

The best things in life is free...

....

....

....

....

....

....

....

....

My Life in chapters

Title of your book:

<u>Chapters of your book</u> -

Chapter 1:

Chapter 2:

Chapter 3:

Chapter 4:

Chapter 5:

Chapter 6:

Chapter 7:

Chapter 8:

Chapter 9:

Chapter 10.

Chapter 11.

Chapter 12:

Where am I?

Year	Weight	Yearly Income	Job

Future self

Year   Where would you like to be:

....

....

....

....

....

....

....

....

....

....

....

....

....

....

Top 10 lists

Movies

1.

2.

3.

4.

5.

6.

7.

8.

9.

10.

TV shows

1.

2.

3.

4.

5.

6.

7.

8.

9.

10.

Singers/bands

1.

2.

3.

4.

5.

6.

7.

8.

9.

10.

Books

1.

2.

3.

4.

5.

6.

7.

8.

9.

10.

Games

1.

2.

3.

4.

5.

6

7.

8.

9.

10.

Hot Celebs

1.

2.

3.

4.

5

6.

7.

8.

9.

10.

Any?

Any addictions?

....

....

....

....

Any lucky charms?

....

....

....

Any regrets?

....

....

....

....

Any habits?

....

....

....

....

Any guilty pleasures?

....

....

....

....

Any changes you've made?

....

....

....

....

Any traditions?

....

....

....

....

Any inventions you would make?

....

....

....

....

[Write a Song about your Life]

....

....

....

....

....

....

....

....

....

....

....

....

....

....

....

....

Time line of my Life

Date   Special events

....

....

....

....

....

....

....

....

....

....

....

....

....

....

Date   <u>Special events</u>

....

....

....

....

....

....

....

....

....

....

....

....

....

....

....

....

Lessons I've learnt in Life

1.

2.

3.

4.

5.

6.

7.

8.

9.

10.

Favourite quotes

....

....

....

....

....

....

....

....

....

....

....

....

....

....

....

....

Things to add...

....

....

....

....

....

....

....

....

....

....

....

....

....

....

....

Made in the USA
San Bernardino, CA
21 March 2019